SAVANNAH

Text by
Malcolm Bell, Jr.

Photography by
N. Jane Iseley

Savannah, outward bound in May 1819 to become the first steamship to cross the Atlantic. The painting, by John Stobart, is from the collection of Morris Newspaper Corporation.

Savannah

HISTORIC SAVANNAH FOUNDATION, INC.
Savannah, Georgia

This book was first published through the generosity of Charles H. Morris, and Morris Newspaper Corporation. Proceeds from the publication benefit Historic Savannah Foundation's program of historic preservation. This second edition is published by the Foundation.

- *FIFTH PRINTING 1995* -
Printed in Hong Kong
Copyright 1977
By Morris Newspaper Corporation and N. Jane Iseley
ALL RIGHTS RESERVED

Richard Stinely, *Designer*
Douglas M. Eason, *Jacket/Cover Designer*

IN recent years Savannah has become rather fashionable among travel writers, and consequently, with their following. Their surprise and their pleasure at finding an American city so out of the ordinary has been conveyed not only to other writers and other travelers but to Savannahians as well. It is as though a curtain has been pulled aside and a musty window glass wiped clean. The natives are seeing clearly, some for the first time, not an old city but a beautiful one. They join the enthusiastic visitor, marvel at the rhythmic pattern of streets, at the beauty of the parks, at the charm and variety of the buildings and homes, and at the wonder and vitality of the river. Together, it makes them think how it all happened, and moreso, how it happened to stay so much as it was.

Old Savannah is but a part of a grand design. This rhythmic pattern of streets and parks that so quickly catches the fancy of visitors, that has long delighted the trained eye of professional city planners and that now comforts and satisfies most of the natives, is but a segment of a truly remarkable venture in colonization.

Although planning had been going on for several years, the real beginning was a cold November day in 1732 that found James Edward Oglethorpe aboard the small ship *ANN*, an insignificant vessel even as measured by the sheltered but broad reaches of the Thames at Gravesend, just below London, and surely by the vast and open seas she would face on her long voyage to America. This departure from Georgian England carried the hopes and fears of Oglethorpe and his 115 colonists. As well, it

Savannahians chose the eminent sculptor Daniel Chester French to honor their founder James Edward Oglethorpe. Facing south from Chippewa Square, the General keeps a wary eye towards the Spanish in Florida.

carried the high hopes and deep anxieties of an odd assortment of conscientious Englishmen—nobility, clergymen, businessmen of the day who were the Trustees for the Colony of Georgia and who were bound together by a common idealistic purpose where the basic strength was a rare understanding of human values.

Oglethorpe, the leader, was an old soldier who mixed his considerable idealism with a strong and useful military discipline. It was good that he did, for the foremost reason for the colony was to protect the English settlement to the north from the Spanish in Florida to the south. A second reason was commerce, and these two, defense and trade, were typical British reasons for colonization. This prompted the financial backing that came from the crown.

What set Georgia apart to give it the grand design was a third reason, the spirit expressed in the Latin motto of the Trustees—*Non Sibi Sed Allis*—Not for self, but for others. True, *others* did not mean Roman Catholics, for the Trustees were apprehensive of the Spanish 'papists' in Florida. And were you a Yamacraw Indian you might have some doubt that the motto applied to your people despite *your* living in peace amongst the colonists, for, after all, had they not moved in and taken your lands? Yet, the motto *did* have meaning. Many of the colonists were the poor of England, and many were the displaced of other lands. Soon to appear at Oglethorpe's outpost on Yamacraw Bluff were two groups of Jews; one a scarce few from Germany, and the second a larger group from Portugal. Early in the second year came a shipload of oppressed people from Central Europe, the Salzburgers, who were Georgia's first Lutherans. Still more displaced, the industrious, headstrong Moravians came seeking a freedom they had lost in Bohemia. There had been other arrivals, notably, a contingent of Highland Scots who were to settle in the Altamaha lowlands and defend Savannah and the colony from the Spanish. Too, there was John Wesley, a young English cleric who came with brother Charles and two others, and who was to find a new and better way of propagating the gospel.

Thus, on Savannah's sandy streets in those early days a visitor would have been an eye-witness to a colorful demonstration of the forging of a new existence in a new found land. For, with the English, the Jews, the Scots, the Salzburgers, the Moravians, there was a scattering of Piedmontese, Swiss, Greeks, and looking on were any number of American Indians—Creeks, Chickasaws, Uchees, Yamasees, and the true native Savannahians, Tomochichi and his Yamacraws. There would be a few Irish and more would come later. Were this before 1749 there would be but few blacks, for until then slavery was prohibited. *More* would come later. But on that day the visitor would be a part of a panorama that portrayed a remarkable manifestation of freedom, and one that foretold the move to American independence.

Savannahians were to rise in anger against their English forebears well before the Declaration of Independence, and were fighting them long after the surrender of Cornwallis at Yorktown. This antagonism against the mother country is rather surprising for Savannah, despite its broad mix of peoples, was very English. Oglethorpe had been a benevolent leader, and James Wright, the Royal Governor at the time of the Revolution, was a good and conscientious man. True, many were loyal to the Crown, yet the taste of freedom given those who were so recently put upon in the British Isles and in Europe and the sense of accomplishment won in a hard new

Savannah has been called the Forest City. Seen from above, the city stretches out along the gently bending river and the green of its many trees is quite evident.

land engendered a determination that would brook no threat of a restrictive, intolerant government. Georgians joined the other English colonies in revolt.

The Georgia colony had lost some of its idealism when the prohibition of slavery was revoked over the protestations of Oglethorpe. Both before and after the Revolution black Africans were brought to Savannah by the thousands and were to color the ways and the speech of its people. They were to have a tremendous effect on the city's commerce, and were to jolt its destiny. Freedom *would* come to these people, but it would come, oh, so much later.

Today's Savannahians and today's visitors can view a city that holds firmly to its past. The great river, although deepened and directed by the Corps of Engineers, still swings close by the city in a sweeping curve and is just as vital as it was in Oglethorpe's day. The stone ballast brought in sailing ships to the new world from the old holds back the sandy bluff and covers the surface of the ramps from the city to the water front, lending a picturesque old-world look that has become one of Savannah's distinguishing features.

Oglethorpe's exalted city plan is surprisingly intact. His squares are downtown gardens offering sunlight and shade to a receptive city. A few have been lost to poor trusteeship on the part of city fathers. Ellis Square, that became a bustling colorful city market in a grand and spacious building is now a shabby parking garage. The three small squares on Montgomery Street were bisected and destroyed. A few short streets have been closed for one reason or another, but thanks to many stalwart Savannahians the original plan is wonderfully unimpaired.

The old town's inventory of fine homes and buildings has been depleted by fire, by storm, neglect, indifference and by occasional misguided self

North Side of Bay Street
   When cotton ruled supreme Bay Street offices became 'Factors Row', a name now lost to 'Factors Walk', a level just beneath Bay Street. Here the arched windows of Stoddard's Upper Range make a dramatic contrast in a rectangular city.

Lutheran Church of the Ascension

Savannah's Lutherans stem from the Salzburgers who first came to Georgia in 1734. The church was founded in 1741 as a hospice and as a place of worship for the faithful who visited the city from their homes at Ebenezer on the Savannah River. The handsome church on Wright Square was dedicated in 1844, the beautiful Ascension window installed by enthusiastic church members in 1878.

interest. The demolition of the city market in 1954 awakened a few Savannahians to what was being irretrievably lost, and there followed a move to stem the destructive tide. Fortunately, the old part of Savannah had remained the core of the city's day-to-day existence. Business was there—scattered around the downtown area and along the Bay. Broughton Street was the only significant retail shopping center. The State and Federal Court Houses buttressed Wright Square. Entertainment was found in the movie theatres and at the old city auditorium, food and lodging at downtown restaurants and hotels. Most important of all, the churches were firmly anchored on their trust lots facing Oglethorpe's squares. Here together was an invaluable heritage from the past—all of the essentials that make a city viable. Yet, Savannah was letting it get away and seemed unwilling to change its course. Following the destruction of the old market there came realization. First a few individuals pointed the way. The Hansell Hillyers led the Savannah Gas Company into restoration of their 'Old Fort' property in a rare example of corporate forethought. Then Historic Savannah Foundation came into being to save the Davenport House. The venerable Telfair Academy of Arts and Sciences inherited a masterpiece unlike any in its extensive collection. This was a magnificent Regency house, the work of the young English architect William Jay. Telfair's careful, meticulous treatment of this inheritance came to be not only a restoration of a fine building but a restoration of a spirit too long dormant in Savannah. Historic Savannah Foundation picked up this spirit to become the single most important force in the restoration movement. This was dramatically demonstrated when the Foundation stayed the housewrecker's hand to rescue the handsome Marshall Row on Oglethorpe Avenue.

The spirit was contagious. Girl Scouters restored the birthplace of their founder, Juliette Gordon Low. The Lane family saved doomed houses by moving them across town, restored neglected squares, and rescued much of the northeast sector of the old town. The ladies of the Trustee's Garden Club turned their considerable talents to abused park areas—the great green strand along the bay that was threatened with black topping, and the quiet beauty of Colonial Cemetery.

Old Savannah is now very much a part of the present. Once again it has become a place for living and the old houses have become new homes for young and old, native and newcomer.

Savannah's heritage from the past is not alone unique architecture, a classic city plan and a busy river. Here, midway into our third century the tolerance, the spiritual freedom, the great mix of peoples are much in evidence. Were General Oglethorpe, the old soldier, and John Wesley, his chaplain, here today they would be rather pleased to see so much intact. Were the General to attend church on the avenue that bears his name hard by the monument that proclaims his greatness he might well find his beloved Scots properly kilted and tartaned. And were John Wesley to attend church he would find the Anglicans, now called Episcopalians, singing his own and brother Charles' hymns. Or perhaps he might choose a church where his own Methodism had taken root. Both would note the well entrenched progeny of their Salzburger friends, would be somewhat surprised at the number of Roman Catholics, so many of them of Irish descent, and both would lament the absence of Indians.

Both would approve the freedom won by the blacks. The General would be secretly pleased, John Wesley would frown on Savannah's fondness for the friendly glass; and, now would be a proper time to drink a toast to the brave General and all he gave us.

John Wesley

The founder of Methodism came to Savannah as a young man fired with a missionary's zeal. He intended to convert the noble savage to Christianity and to minister the Anglican gospel to the colonists. Twenty three months later he returned to England a changed and chastened man. He had lost his heart and the girl he loved, had found the Indian more savage than noble, and with few exceptions, the colonists unable to receive his Christian message. Yet, the fire was not extinguished and was to burn until his death fifty years later in the widespread evangelical movement that became Methodism.

Savannah River

It was the river that gave the town its beautiful name and it is the river that is Savannah's greatest reason for being. Oglethorpe chose well when he decided on the high land above the 'bluff' on a graceful crescent of the river a scant fifteen miles from the sea. Today massive cargo vessels have replaced the handsome sailing ships that once filled the harbor. Their superstructures rise high above the five-storied buildings along the bay just as did the masts of sailing ships in the days gone by.

When steam power began its inevitable replacement of sail, the Savannah River became much a part of the change. In 1819, the small, valiant *Savannah* steamed down the river to become the first of her kind to venture and succeed in an ocean crossing.

Now a general cargo port, Savannah in the past has seen great shipments of lumber, cotton, rice, naval stores and paper.

The Waving Girl

For 45 years Florence Martus greeted ships by night and day from her brother's lonely cottage on an island in the river. A legend now, and in her time, her park below the harbor light is an attractive place from which to view the busy river.

City Hall and its four-sided clock tower seen from the island across the main channel of the river

An inbound ship heads upstream to discharge cargo at one of the city's busy terminals.

City Hall is seen from town-side with a jaunty tug headed up-stream.

Many of the buildings that appear to be two stories high on Bay Street become an impressive five stories on River Street. Their once useful balconies are being refurbished now that the new esplanade has come to the waterfront.

Old World Stone

Sailing ships bound to Savannah for cargo often carried stone as ballast. When stone cast into the river caused shoaling the ships were required to discharge their ballast ashore. In the 1850's it was put to good use in surfacing the ramps leading down to the river, and in containing the sandy bluff that had plagued Savannahians since Oglethorpe's day.

The old Cotton Exchange is now Freemasons Hall and is flanked by office buildings that face the handsome strand along the Bay and back up to the river below.

The fountain in Emmet Park along the Bay pays tribute to three ships named *Savannah*; the first steamship to cross the Atlantic, the gallant World War II cruiser, and the pioneer nuclear cargo ship built to demonstrate the peaceful uses of atomic power.

The old anchors were lost by sailing ships and were recovered by dredging operations that widen and deepen the harbor.

206 West Bay Street
Imaginative Savannahians have converted an old warehouse to an attractive residence with a spectacular view of the river.

The New Waterfront
   In a city renowned for its parks, the new esplanade along the waterfront has a sweeping view of the river giving promise of becoming for Savannah what Charleston's High Battery has been for so many years.

Bull Street

Few cities are graced with any thoroughfare quite so fine as the short stretch of Bull Street between City Hall on the Bay and Forsyth Park twenty blocks to the south. Named for the South Carolinian, Colonel William Bull, who befriended the colonists, the street winds around five of Savannah's most beautiful squares and is the focal point of Oglethorpe's grand design. The squares display handsome monuments to an original Savannahian, Tomochichi, Mico of the Yamacraws; to Oglethorpe; and to three stalwart soldiers of the Revolution; General Nathanael Greene, the Irish-American patriot Sergeant William Jasper, and the courageous Polish volunteer, Casimir Pulaski. Jasper and Pulaski were both killed in the bitter, bloody fighting at the abortive Siege of Savannah when the British, defending the town, fought off combined French and American forces. One monument pays tribute to William W. Gordon who founded the Central Railroad.

Along Bull Street are the churches where congregations have long created a cohesive variety so much a part of the city's character. Most face the squares from their trust lots. Also along the street are many of Savannah's important buildings including the dignified U. S. Custom House, several banks, the Federal and State Court Houses, a building that has become a mecca-like shrine to thousands of American Girl Scouts, and many handsome old residences.

The Washington Guns and the U.S. Custom House

President Washington visited Savannah in 1791 and presented the Chatham Artillery with a pair of brass cannon captured from the British at Yorktown. These handsome guns are displayed on the Bay and have been used to salute many presidents who have followed Washington to Savannah. In the background is the U. S. Custom House completed in 1852 on the site of Oglethorpe's cabin. The great columns each weigh 15 tons and were quarried at Quincy, Massachusetts and brought to Savannah by sailing ship. The fine hand of architect John S. Norris, who designed the building, is many times evident in Savannah.

Johnson Square

The stone shaft designed by William Strickland pays tribute to and marks the grave of General Nathanael Greene. The square is named for Governor William Johnson of South Carolina who gave Oglethorpe a helping hand. Savannah's first square, it has always been the keystone of the planned city and the most vital of its parks.

Christ Church

The imposing Greek Revival building completed in 1838 is the third church to face Johnson Square from the southeast trust lot. Anglican until after the Revolution and thereafter Episcopalian, Christ Church has been led by men such as John Wesley and George Whitefield. Its parishioners have long figured prominently in the history and development of the city.

Bull Street

In a camera-foreshortened view looking north from a point just south of Wright Square are monuments to William W. Gordon who led the development of the Central of Georgia Railroad; Nathanael Greene in Johnson Square, and the domed clock tower of City Hall on the Bay.

In Wright Square

Tomichichi, Oglethorpe's friend, and leader of the Yamacraws is remembered by Savannahians with this great granite rock from North Georgia.

Juliette Gordon Low Birthplace

Girl Scouts from all across America have made the pilgrimage to the birthplace of their founder Juliette Gordon Low. Beautifully restored and furnished the house is a fitting tribute to a remarkable woman. The house was built in 1820 for the distinguished Savannah jurist and Mayor of the City, James Moore Wayne. Some historians attribute the design to the young English architect, William Jay.

Independent Presbyterian Church

President Monroe came to Savannah in 1819, journeyed to Tybee Island at the mouth of the Savannah River, on the new steamship *Savannah*. He was honored at a ball in William Jay's pavilion in Johnson Square and participated in the dedication of the Independent Presbyterian Church. The towering steeple has long been a Savannah landmark, and the grand design of the building by John Holden Greene, A Rhode Island architect, is marked by fine exterior details and a classic sun-lit interior.

First Baptist Church

Savannah's oldest Baptist congregation has worshipped on Chippewa Square since 1833 and no downtown church brings more suburbanites to the old part of town than does First Baptist.

Wetter House Iron Work

Had Historic Savannah Foundation been on the scene the destruction of the monumental Wetter House on Oglethorpe Avenue would not have occurred. The house, surrounded as it was by heavy Gothic cast iron, was dramatic in appearance and its loss to a used car lot was inexcusable.

The medallioned panels were saved and a few are shown here on Chippewa Square.

St. John's Parish House

   The parish house for St. John's Episcopal Church was first the home of cotton merchant Charles Green. It was designed and built in 1853 by John S. Norris. When union forces captured Savannah in 1864, General William T. Sherman made the house his headquarters. The Gothic style complements the church and lends a pleasant variation to the architecture around Madison Square.

4 West Taylor Street
An example of the remarkable ornamental ironwork to be found on the houses that surround Monterey Square.

Monterey Square
The southern-most of the Bull Street squares is the center of one of old Savannah's most agreeable residential neighborhoods.

10 West Taylor Street
    A Taylor Street house shows exuberant iron work and a striking ornamental facade.

Temple Mickve Israel
   Savannah's oldest Jewish congregation, the Mickve Israel was founded in July 1733 and has been worshipping from the temple on Monterey Square since 1878. George Washington called on the "wonder-working Deity" to water the congregation "with the dews of heaven."

The Pulaski Monument
    An allegorical figure of Liberty tops the towering marble shaft that honors the memory of the Polish soldier Casimir Pulaski who lost his life in a vain attempt to wrest Savannah from British control.

Hugh Mercer House—429 Bull Street

Another house associated with Norris, this one Italianate, brings more variety to Monterey Square. Few Savannah houses have been restored so well, or furnished so grandly.

The colorful domelight brightens the graceful stairway.

Forsyth Park
 The park is loveliest in early spring when azaleas and flowing trees come into bloom. The park and its fountain are a proper turning point for a walk out Bull Street.

423 Bull Street
  The Italian fountain is in the garden of the northern-most Charles Rogers house.

Late Eighteenth-Century Houses

507 East St. Julian Street

There are but few gambrel roof houses in old Savannah although this, the Hamptom Lillibridge House, once had a neighbor quite similar in appearance and construction. In moving the two from East Bryan Street, one collapsed and was lost. The house was built circa 1796, was said to be haunted but was freed of the supernatural when exorcised by the Episcopal Bishop.

510 East St. Julian Street
   This cottage was built in 1797 as the home of Major Charles Odingsells, a soldier of the Revolution and a farmer, who died on Skidaway Island and is buried in Colonial Cemetery.

426 East St. Julian Street
   A small house moved from Price Street to its present site and quite typical of the first houses in which most colonists lived. A very few have survived the fires, the storms, and changing neighborhoods.

24 Habersham Street

John David Mongin, cotton planter and merchant, built this Federal style house in 1797 on the southwest corner of Congress and Habersham Streets. Moved across the street in 1964 the house continues to look out on Warren Square, and both, house and square are enjoying a new lease on life. The garden behind the house brightens this attractive corner.

122 East Oglethorpe Avenue
 One of Savannah's earliest houses, this cottage was built in the 1760's and raised above its brick lower story in the 1870's. The flag stone sidewalks along the avenue prevailed when Savannah's streets were either sandy wastes or muddy quagmires.

William Jay

In December 1817 the ship *Dawn* arrived in Savannah from England heralding a bright new day for Savannah architecture. Aboard was a young English architect, 23 years old. His father, a dissident minister of Bath was to write of his son that while he had "professional talent and cleverness" he also had "a large share of wit and humour, qualities always dangerous and commonly injurious to the possessor."

The Jay houses and buildings were Savannah's finest. Alas! Much is now gone.

Owens-Thomas House

The finest of the Jay houses in Savannah is the Regency house on Oglethorpe Square, completed in 1819 for Richard Richardson, President of the Savannah Branch of the Bank of the United States. Miss Margaret Thomas bequeathed her home to the Telfair Academy in 1951. Telfair's restoration was done with proper attention to Jay's beautiful design. The graceful portico is but an introduction to the startlingly handsome and imaginative interior.

The young architect's eye for form and dimension is evident in every room, his treatment of this space being mindful of the style of the English Regency architect, Sir John Soane.

The cast iron porch on the President Street side of the house is graced with delicate Corinthian columns. Here in 1825 Lafayette stood to speak to assembled Savannahians.

The green grass and live oaks of Oglethorpe Square give a town house a country dimension.

The beauty of Oglethorpe Square in front is complemented by a formal garden between the house and the carriage houses at the rear.

William Scarbrough House

Completed in time for a grand reception honoring President James Monroe in May, 1819, this magnificent house further demonstrates the remarkable talents of William Jay. Saved and restored by Historic Savannah Foundation, the house was long used as an elementary school for negro children.

Trinity Methodist Church and Telfair Academy

Telfair Square on Barnard Street is flanked on the west by John B. Hogg's Trinity Church and by William Jay's Telfair Academy of Arts and Sciences.

The rapid growth of the Methodist congregation in Savannah led to the construction of Trinity Church in 1848. The seeds planted by John Wesley had found fertile ground.

The square had first been called St. James', named for London's royal residence. Three royal governors including Sir James Wright had lived on the northwest trust lot where Jay was to design the grand residence of Alexander Telfair who was to live there with his two sisters, Margaret and Mary. In 1875 Mary willed the family home to Savannah to become a museum. That it is today, a fine art museum where a rather remarkable collection of paintings is shown in a setting few galleries can match.

The beauty of this long room with its rounded ends is enhanced by fine Telfair furniture including a superb circular expandable dining table.

A favorite of Jay's, this great segmental arched window throws sunlight to the entrance hall below.

Colonial Cemetery

In 1758 the Province of Georgia was divided into parishes. At the time the town's burial ground became the parish cemetery for Christ Church yet by custom remained the public graveyard. In 1895 the city reacquired the hallowed ground and gave jurisdiction to the Park and Tree Commission. Ravaged by neglect and by vandals, the cemetery is at last given the respect it is due. Now, the living and the dead find the cemetery a place to rest in peace.

The Pink House

Many of Savannah's fine homes owe their salvation to a conversion to commercial use. This late 18th century building was first the home of James Habersham, Jr. and in 1812 became the Planters Bank. Its present-day use is as a restaurant and tavern, long popular with visitors and natives alike. With its neighbor to the south, the Oliver Sturges House, the two are all that is left of the past on Reynolds Square.

Oliver Sturges House

In 1813 Oliver Sturges and Benjamin Burroughs constructed a pair of houses on the trust lot facing Reynolds Square on land originally set aside for the parsonage of Christ Church. John Wesley and George Whitefield had lived and tended their flock in the earlier building. The Burroughs house has been lost, but there is no more interesting restoration in the old town than that bestowed upon the Sturges house. Here the epic voyage of the steamship *Savannah* was planned, the beginning of which is graphically captured in the painting by John Stobart. The house is now headquarters for Morris Newspaper Corporation, the adaptation from residence to office having been accomplished with skill and good taste.

Isaiah Davenport House

Threatened destruction of the Davenport house on Columbia Square gave impetus to the formation of Historic Savannah Foundation. Stalwart Savannah women rallied to the cause, saved the house in 1954 and since that day the Foundation has become the greatest force in the city's preservation movement.

Isaiah Davenport was a Rhode Islander who brought New England ideas and methods to Savannah. A master builder, he designed and built his own house in the Federal style. The house has been headquarters for the Foundation and is now a beautifully furnished house museum.

The cast iron downspouts with the open-mouthed dolphin were once rather numerous in old Savannah. Most have disappeared, but walkers will notice a few, and as well, a new and grand model fashioned by a local iron worker.

A grandly ornate interior belies the graceful simplicity of the Davenport facade.

Aaron Champion House—230 Barnard Street

Charles Cluskey, Irish born architect, left his mark on Savannah and a good mark it is. Facing Orleans Square from the southeast trust lot, the Aaron Champion house, is a robust Greek revival with a particularly dramatic entrance hall.

Big Duke and 113 East Oglethorpe Avenue

Big Duke sounded fire alarms from a steel tower that rose high above Colonial Cemetery. Now the tip of the tower and the huge bell are in Oglethorpe Avenue's median in front of the fire house, and the bell sounds only on special occasions.

The avenue was originally South Broad Street, the southern extremity of the town. The house on the avenue is an interesting mix of masonry and frame construction with second floor and third floor porches offering shade and cool breezes in by-gone summers. Savannah's porch sitters disappeared when air conditioning arrived.

Oglethorpe Avenue

The south side of Oglethorpe Avenue presents an interesting assortment of styles. The paired houses on the right were built in the early 1820's as the town moved beyond its original confines.

Mary Marshall Row

    On the north side of Oglethorpe Avenue across from Colonial Cemetery are the four houses of Mary Marshall Row. Built in the mid 1850's, generous in dimension, the houses are made of Savannah gray brick, and though the arrangement of double pairs differs from the usual row, the Marshall houses have a distinctive *Savannah* look.

    The high price of Savannah gray brick led the owners to contract for demolition in 1959. Historic Savannah Foundation saved the buildings after carriage houses in the rear were actually coming down.

The corner house of Marshall Row has been beautifully restored by Georgians who have returned to Savannah from foreign service with the U. S. State Department. The scenic wallpaper, an adaptation of a 19th century design, was handpainted in Paris.

The Cathedral of John the Baptist
The Cathedral for Savannah's numerous Roman Catholics is an imposing twin-towered church on Lafayette Square. Begun in 1872 and designed by Baltimore architect E. Francis Baldwin, the building was faced in Savannah gray brick. In 1898 a spectacular fire caused extensive damage and it was in the following reconstruction that the burned brick were covered with white stucco.

116 East McDonough Street
    The brownstone arch and fanlighted opening above the doorway lend a graceful touch to this Savannah gray brick house built by Matthew Lufburrow in 1831.

119 East Charlton Street
    The well-tended formal garden was very much a part of old Savannah. Edged in tile, ornamental brick, or round bottom bottles the flower beds were intricate in design and might be green, colorful or fragrant, or all three at once.
    The William Battersby House, 1852, is entered through the side verandah, a rare example of the Charleston style in Savannah. The garden is one of the city's loveliest.

The Colonial Dames House

Andrew Low, cotton merchant of Liverpool and Savannah built his Lafayette Square mansion in 1849. It is thought that John S. Norris was the designer. Here lived Andrew Low's daughter-in-law Juliette Gordon Low and it was here in 1912 that she founded the first Girl Scout Troop in America. Acquired by the Colonial Dames in 1928, the house is restored and furnished in the grand manner, and is open to the public.

The carriage house in the rear was a gift to Savannah Girl Scouts from Mrs. Low.

William Makepeace Thackeray, friend of Andrew Low, visited Savannah in 1855. From this upstairs bedroom he wrote his notes of the "tranquil old city, wide-streeted, tree-planted."

Troup Square

Savannah's squares are of varying sizes. Troup Square on Habersham Street is comparatively small but this gives an extra dimension to its four trust lots. On the eastern side are two remarkable restorations, the Troup Trust and McDonough Row. The buildings of the Trust are seen from the square that is graced by a striking armillary.

Jones Street

In the Savannah plan the east-west streets midway between the squares were given more generous dimensions. Broughton, Oglethorpe, Liberty and Jones are all wider than other cross-town streets.

The houses on Jones Street are sheltered by live oaks that often meet above to form an evergreen canopy. The street has an interesting mix of true mansions, high and low stoops, paired houses and frame dwellings of assorted design and size.

The 100 block of West Jones Street is fairly typical and is the site of one of Historic Savannah Foundation's successful reclamation efforts.

11 East Jones Street
   Much of Jones Street is paved in hard red brick, a material once popular for street surfaces in Savannah but now replaced by asphalt and concrete. This free-standing house dates from the early 1850's and was built by John Scudder, a master mason who migrated to Savannah from New Jersey in the early 19th century.

Whitefield Square
 Whitefield Square is Habersham Street's southern-most. The whimsical gazebo is most appropriate for many of the houses in the neighborhood

reflect the gingerbread fashion that swept through America at the turn of the century. Again appropriately, Whitefield Square is in Wesley Ward, the names honoring the two colonial clerics.

Massie School

Peter Massie, a Scottish migrant to Georgia, concerned himself with the uneducated poor of Savannah. He gave the city money and provided the incentive to build what became Savannah's first public school. Facing Calhoun Square, the school was designed by the busy John S. Norris and was opened in 1856. Norris was responsible for the center section, the wings having been added in 1872 and 1886. Massie was an active school for 118 years and is now a center for training where relics of its historic past are on display.

508-12 East Bryan Street
  Savannah's penchant for row houses occasionally carries over from brick to latter-day frame construction. In the 1890's these low-stoop houses were built in one of the towns older neighborhoods. Today they offer comfortable downtown living.

Gordon Row, 101-129 West Gordon Street

    The fifteen houses on Gordon Row cover the block between Whitaker and Barnard Streets where several of the houses face Chatham Square. The row is surprisingly intact, even to the carriage or garden houses in the rear. Built in 1853, the seemingly narrow 20-foot width of each house is overcome by a generous depth and vertical dimension. The strong gracefully curved cast iron stair railings in front and many attractive gardens in back help to keep these houses very much in demand.

20 West Gaston Street

Gaston Street marks the southern extremity of Savannah's design under the continuation of Oglethorpe's original town plan. These houses face Forsyth Park, the handsome one in the foreground being another fine example of John S. Norris' architecture.

East Gaston Street

  A view looking to the West along Gaston Street. Savannah, hot in the summer, has long valued its shade trees. The Park and Tree Commission, stubbornly to some, and courageously to others, defends its charges—the city trees and parks. The Commission is traditionally non-political.

Hodgson Hall

Named for Margaret Telfair's scholarly husband, William Brown Hodgson, the Hall is the home, library and archives of the venerable Georgia Historical Society. The building was designed by the New York architect Detlief Lienau, was dedicated in 1876, a gift to the Society from Mrs. Hodgson and her sister Mary Telfair.

Hodgson Hall is listed on the National Register of Historic Places in recognition of its rare architectural and historic values.

The Central of Georgia

1843 was a significant year for Savannah and the state. The town's considerable maritime commerce was tied to the new railroad that reached out into the rich farm lands of Georgia and the effect was dramatic. Along the line villages were to become towns and towns became cities.

In Savannah the Central was the most important industry. The station on West Broad Street was but part of a vital railroad complex that included shops, offices, warehouses, terminals, yards and a great network of tracks.

The train shed, now a part of Savannah's Visitors Center is used for art festivals and community gatherings. The station building is headquarters for the Chamber of Commerce. Before the automobile came into fashion the Central Station was the most exciting and busiest place in town.

Fort Jackson

On the river, just downstream from Savannah and close by the inland passage to Carolina and to Florida, is a small masonry fort named for the Georgia patriot James Jackson. Begun in 1842 on the site of earlier fortifications, Fort Jackson is just above Five Fathom Hole where sailing ships were frequently off-loaded and lightened in order that they might navigate the shallow Savannah River to the town.

Restored by the Georgia Historical Commission in 1965 the fort is now maintained by the Coastal Heritage Society.

Fort Pulaski

When John Wesley first kneeled to pray in the new world it was on Peeper's Island at the mouth of the Savannah River. In 1829 when construction had begun on a massive fortification designed by the French military engineer Simon Bernard, the island had taken the name of a useless and troublesome plant that thrived there, the cockspur.

The Fort on Cockspur Island was to be the last word in military construction. The best brains of the Corps of Engineers had modified Bernard's design and their best

men supervised its building. One of these was the young Lt. Robert E. Lee, fresh from West Point on his first assignment. In a sense the Fort proved to be the last word for early in the Civil War Federal troops breached the great walls with ease by using a new weapon, the rifled cannon. The Fort was swiftly captured.

Today, an easily accessible national monument, Fort Pulaski is an amazingly spectacular example of military architecture. 25,000,000 bricks were used to exacting specifications by masons of rare skill and talent.

Isle of Hope

    Savannahians long sought respite from sultry summers by finding homes along the tidal rivers between the city and the sea. The Isle of Hope was, and is, a favorite community on the salt water. The gracious homes are well designed for cool breezes in the shadow of live oaks with a ready view of the river and the islands beyond.

Wormsloe

    Wormsloe, on the Isle of Hope was granted to colonist Noble Jones by the Georgia trustees and the house is owned by his descendants today. The formal garden near the house is surrounded by a magnificent grove of ancient live oaks.

Thunderbolt
 Shrimp boats find a haven beneath the bluff on the Wilmington River at the picturesque fishing village of Thunderbolt.

A blind beacon, long abandoned, marks the entrance to the south channel of the Savannah River.